What if we do

nOTHING?

RAINFOREST DESTRUCTION

Ewan McLeish

FRANKLIN WATTS
LONDON•SYDNEY

First published in 2007 by
Franklin Watts
338 Euston Road
London NW1 3BH

Franklin Watts Australia
Hachette Children's Books
Level 17/207 Kent St, Sydney, NSW 2000

Produced by Arcturus Publishing Limited,
26/27 Bickels Yard, 151-153 Bermondsey Street, London SE1 3HA

Series concept: Alex Woolf
Editor: Jenni Rainford
Designer: Peta Phipps
Consultant: Rob Bowden

Picture Credits
Corbis: 5 (RICKEY ROGERS/Reuters/Corbis), 6 (Vic Kintanar/epa/Corbis),
9 (Tony Arruza/CORBIS), 10 (Zainal Abd Halim/Reuters/Corbis), 12 (Joel Creed; Eye
Ubiquitous/CORBIS), 15 and cover (Kazuyoshi Nomachi/CORBIS), 16 and cover (Karen
Kasmauski/CORBIS), 19 (Joe McDonald/CORBIS), 20 (Renee Lynn/CORBIS),
25 (Reuters / Corbis), 29 (Reuters/CORBIS), 30 (Colin MacPherson/Colin McPherson/
Corbis), 33 (Janet Jarman/Corbis), 35 (Bob Krist/Corbis), 37 (Reuters/CORBIS),
38 (David A. Northcott/CORBIS), 41 (Wolfgang Kaehler/CORBIS),
42 (Dan Lamont/CORBIS).
Rex Features: 22 (Lehtikuva OY/Rex Features), 26 and cover (Paul Raffaele/Rex
Features), 44 (Patrick Frillet/Rex Features).

A CIP catalogue record for this book is available from the British Library

Dewey Decimal Classification Number: 333.75

ISBN: 978 0 7496 6966 9

Printed in China

Contents

CHAPTER 1

Paradise Lost

It is 2045 and most of the world's tropical rainforests have disappeared. Those that remain are either protected in nature reserves or are now too small to support the huge range of animals and plants that once lived there. Much of what was once great rainforest has turned to desert. The soil that for millions of years was protected by the roots of the giant forest trees has been washed away. Now the farms that replaced the forests are gone. Landslides constantly engulf village communities, and even towns and cities, as great seas of mud slip and slither down the treeless mountain and hillsides.

Over 50 percent of all land animal and plant species may be extinct by the year 2045. Many of the indigenous (native) people may have gone due to disease or simply because their rainforest way of life could no longer be sustained. As the land deteriorates, poor farmers may flock to the cities to find jobs, but if there are too many farmers and not enough jobs, this may cause anxiety and rioting over high unemployment.

How could this happen?

It could happen if, for decades, groups of people clear the rainforests for their timber, land and mineral needs, carving great roads across them and leaving them exposed to further exploitation. And if they fail to replace the cleared trees, much of the stripped earth would never recover.

The consequences

These possible consequences are serious and frightening. Rainforests cover about 6 million square kilometres – an area about three-quarters the size of Australia. Though there are some rainforests that are so remote that they are unlikely to be destroyed by clearing, currently rainforests are being destroyed at a rate of about 32,000 hectares a day, or nearly 12 million hectares (120,000 square kilometres) a year. If you divide the area of rainforest that is left (6 million square kilometres) by the annual rate in square kilometres at which they are being destroyed (120,000 square kilometres) you get the number of years left before almost all have gone, if we do nothing – 50 years.

Types of forest

There are different types of rainforest: tropical rainforests (which this book deals with) receive large amounts of rainfall all the year round, whereas boreal temperate rainforests are cooler and found north and south of the two tropics, in countries such as Canada, the United States and Russia.

This rainforest in the Amazon Basin has been cleared by loggers. In 40 or 50 years' time, if we continue to destroy rainforests at the current rate, this could be all that is left of most of them.

Tropical rainforests extend from the Equator to the tropics. Not surprisingly, they are much warmer than temperate rainforests and contain the greatest diversity of life in any land habitat. Primary rainforest is original, natural forest; secondary rainforest is where replanting has occurred.

OVERALL RATES OF TROPICAL DEFORESTATION*

	Total forest cover (2005)		Total deforestation
	1000 hectares	% total land area	(% loss since 1990)
Central America	22,411	43.9	-18.9
South America	831,540	47.7	-6.7
Southeast Asia	283,127	33.4	-12.4
Australasia and Pacific (Oceania)	206,254	24.3	-2.9
Africa	559,000	34.3	-9.9

*NB these figures are for the regions as a whole; some of these losses will be for other types of forest, although the majority is rainforest.

Source: mongabay/FAO/CFAN

Mountains on the move

On February 17, 2006, a mudslide swept down the mountainsides above the farming village of Guinsaugon in the Philippines. Villagers were buried beneath the thick, glutinous mud and 1,800 were killed. An entire school was also swept away. Many reasons were given for the disaster: there had been prolonged rains and the region was unstable anyway. Many blamed the clearing of forests high above the buried village because, with nothing to hold the soil in place, there was nothing to hold the mountain in place either.

Rescue workers confront scenes of total devastation after a landslip engulfed a village in the Philippines in 2005. Images like this may become increasingly common as forest cover on hillsides is removed, allowing landslides to destroy towns and villages.

A freak event?

Sadly, this was not an isolated event. Many villages on the islands that make up Indonesia in Southeast Asia are also repeatedly devastated by landslides and mudslips. Indonesia has some of the most aggressive logging policies in the world, with whole areas of forest being stripped of trees.

This may seem like the kind of thing you hear about on the news every other day, but we have to take notice: the problem won't go away if we stop thinking about it. But we first need to understand why rainforest destruction happens. We need to understand that it is not always about carelessness or greed, but about the poverty and needs of the people involved, and that there are no simple solutions.

Can we stop it now? Further loss is inevitable, even if decisive action were taken today. Our best hope is to reduce the rate at which the destruction is taking place and then gradually turn the situation around. It is not solely the responsibility of others or governments on the other side of the world: we all have a role to play. We may not want our children, or their children, to ask, 'Why did you do nothing?'

DEBATE

You are concerned that most of the world's rainforests may disappear in your lifetime. You want your school to run a one-day debate on the future of rainforests. How do you convince your teachers that this would be a worthwhile idea?

- You argue that debating real issues that affect the future of yourself and others is a key aspect of your education.
- You argue that there won't *be* much of a future if we ignore issues like the destruction of rainforests.

CHAPTER 2

Rainforests in Retreat

It is 2020 and rainforests are now being attacked on all sides. A number of world organizations are meeting to discuss the state of the world's rainforests as an urgent priority. The meeting is being hosted by the United Nations Environment Programme (UNEP), but other organizations involved include the World Resources Institute, and the Food and Agriculture Organization (FAO), together with the the World Bank. Some delegates have protested at the presence of the World Bank at this meeting, as they believe that the Bank's policies support large-scale 'development' projects, such as dam and road construction, which allow poor countries to build up huge debts. They criticize the World Bank's representatives for having contributed to the problem they are there to discuss. Others think it is too late for blame. As one senior delegate puts it, "We all have to work together now; if we don't get it right this time, we will not get another chance."

Getting behind the headlines

Before looking at the real causes of rainforest destruction, it is important to understand some of the factors that create situations in which deforestation can occur. In 2000 the population of the world was 6 billion; by 2013 it is estimated that it will be 7 billion, and by 2028, 8 billion. Much of this increase is occurring in poor or rapidly developing countries – such as those in parts of South America, Africa and Asia – that are least able to deal with the increase. Many of these people are, or will be, living in extreme poverty. Poverty is not a 'cause' of deforestation but it creates a situation in which people are forced to take desperate measures in order to survive. This may include destroying their own environment, for example, by farming rainforest land in ways that cause permanent damage to the soil.

Debt is also a factor, as many poor or developing countries owe large amounts of money to banks and other agencies in the richer countries. Most find it hard just to keep up with interest payments. Some of these debts are in the process of being written off, but the basic problem remains. Like poor people, poor countries are forced to take short-term measures, like exploiting their forests for timber when, in the longer term, they would be more valuable left standing.

Low-income people in Honduras have neither the time nor the resources to look after their land. Soon this land will be useless and the family will move on to clear more forest.

RUNNING TO STAND STILL

Brazil is undergoing an export boom, but its desire to export is driven by its need to pay back its massive foreign debt. Three-quarters of its foreign earnings go in 'servicing' its debt of about US$250 billion. This has put pressure on the country to increase international exports, such as timber, beef and soya, to an all-time high. Therefore there is increased pressure on its rainforests, as they are cleared to facilitate such income-earning activities.

A family matter

Perhaps surprisingly, the single biggest cause of deforestation is the family farm. In the past, farming families, living on or near the edges of forests, would clear the forest margins to plant and grow crops, mainly to feed themselves. Methods were used that were in harmony with the land's ability to recover. Crops were planted to support the farming family, such as corn, beans, cassava and plantains, and long 'fallow' periods were allowed during which no crops were grown. This allowed the soil to regenerate, and the family would move or 'shift' to cultivate a new plot, nearby.

This so-called 'shifting cultivation' did not generally harm the rainforests. In fact, it was sometimes even beneficial as the margins between the forest and the cultivated land provided a new 'niche' that attracted a range of wild animals and plants. The problems came, however, as more and more people were forced by poverty to set up farms at the forest edges. Often they lacked the skills of the

A plantation worker tends oil palm fruits. These yield valuable palm oil that is exported worldwide and used in the manufacture of margarine, cooking oils and biscuits. In Indonesia, palm oil makes up nearly 80 percent of all exports. Although plantations are often located on land already cleared of rainforest, they can still create problems such as pollution of water supplies and loss of wildlife.

traditional shifting cultivators and so the farms failed. The pressure caused by the increasing population even forced the traditional farmers to reduce the fallow period, as there was less and less land available to farm.

In this way, the traditional systems of farming became less sustainable. The old way of shifting cultivation, which had been successful for perhaps thousands of years, became destructive. The forest edges were cleared by cutting and burning: the ash adds valuable plant nutrients to the soil. Crops were planted – traditional varieties, as well as so-called cash crops, such as coffee and citrus fruits – to sell to local buyers. With no time allowed for regeneration, the soil was exhausted within a few years and the farm had to be abandoned. Meanwhile, the family – and hundreds of thousands like them – moved on to clear new forest. It is estimated that these unsustainable farming methods now account for nearly two-thirds of all deforestation. It may seem strange that this way of life can have such a devastating effect on the great rainforests. But a single family may clear enormous areas over a period of time. Also, as we shall see later, rainforest soils themselves are already quite thin and poor in nutrients.

Plantation damage

The much bigger agricultural businesses or 'agribusinesses', such as plantation owners, grow commercial crops, including palm oil, rubber, soya, coffee, cacao and tropical fruits, on huge tracts of land. They have a double effect: firstly, they occupy the best, most fertile soils, usually located in valleys. As a result, rural populations are moved onto less fertile soil or forced to clear new forest in order to survive. Secondly, they clear forested land themselves, often through government-subsidized deals. This type of commercial agriculture may also bring further problems such as contamination of soil with pesticides and damage to the health of farm labourers who use them. In addition, many of these crops require much greater amounts of water than indigenous (local) varieties, resulting in too much water being extracted from the ground.

TOP TEN HIGHEST AVERAGE ANNUAL DEFORESTATION OF PRIMARY FOREST 2000-05

Brazil	34,660 sq km
Indonesia	14,478 sq km
Mexico	3,950 sq km
Papua New Guinea	2,502 sq km
Peru	2,246 sq km
Bolivia	1,352 sq km
Sudan	1,178 sq km
Nigeria	820 sq km
Cambodia	668 sq km
Colombia	561 sq km

Source: FAO/Mongabay

Meanwhile, back at the ranch...

Cattle ranching, especially in Central and South America, is another major cause of deforestation. In the past, ranchers preferred the more easily managed rangelands of dry forest and savannah further from the Equator. Later, they turned their attention to the moist tropical rainforests. Ranchers operate in two main ways. Firstly, they may occupy large tracts of forest and clear the land themselves. Alternatively, they buy up land that has already been cleared by farmers and convert this into pasture. Once the land is converted and fenced, the rancher may sub-lease the land to other farmers, and then move deeper into the forest to repeat the cycle.

Since the 1950s, the area of land under permanent pasture for such practices as ranching, has increased from 3.9 million hectares to 13.4 million hectares in Central America alone. Much of this has been at the expense of the region's tropical rainforest. Ranching is an attractive alternative to other land uses because it is reasonably profitable in the short term, requires little labour and has vast markets, such as the USA and Europe. Some of this demand has

Cattle ranching for the beef market in Central and South America is profitable, but cleared forest soils are fragile and easily damaged by trampling. In the past, beef production was important for the export market, for example, to the USA, Europe and Japan. More recently, however, cattle are being reared for the rapidly growing domestic (home) market, increasing the pressure to clear more land.

GOING UP IN SMOKE

Forest fires destroy or damage between 6 and 14 million hectares of tropical forest every year; that's roughly equal to damage caused by logging and conversion to agriculture combined! Often the fires are started deliberately as a way of illegally clearing more forest. Severe fires in Indonesia in 1997 caused high levels of air pollution, affecting 75 million people overall. Fires have a double impact: they add significantly to carbon dioxide (CO_2) in the atmosphere, while the destruction of rainforests removes their ability to absorb the polluting gases.

been reduced, as people in the richer countries have been made more aware of the damaging effects of their demand for cheap imported beef. But as some of the rainforest countries themselves become wealthier, increasing 'home' demand from within these countries still fuels the beef market at the expense of their forests. In addition, the demand to grow soya for cattle feed is increasing, resulting in the expansion of plantations (see page 11).

Clearing forests for fuel

For most of the world's poor, wood is the only source of fuel available to them – in fact, 80 percent of all wood used worldwide is for fuelwood. Many of those who use fuelwood as a source of energy are the rural poor, and much of what they gather is naturally fallen deadwood. Wood is also a major fuel for urban use, having often been converted into charcoal first. The collection of fuelwood does not necessarily destroy rainforests, but it does cause them to be damaged or degraded. Sometimes the habitat is altered by certain preferred trees being removed. New species may take over but the quality of the woodland is damaged. Around cities and other urban areas there is often a ring of bare land many kilometres wide, as people (especially fuel businesses who convert the wood into charcoal to sell) travel further and further to meet their energy needs.

DEBATE

You are in charge
You are a politician in an African country with large areas of rainforest still standing. You are under pressure from a large multinational company that wants to grow palm oil in a primary forest area. Which of the following courses of action do you take?

- Agree to the plan, but say you will charge them ten times what they are offering for the use of the land.
- Resist the offer and explore the possibility of leasing land that has already been cleared of rainforest.

CHAPTER 3

Timber!

It is 2020 and Enriqué is a government timber inspector for a rainforest country. His job is to monitor the government's sustainable timber programme and ensure that all logs taken from his 'patch' come from rainforests that are properly managed and certified. The job is not going well, however. He knows that illegal logging is still common, even on government-owned land, but it is hard to prove. Enriqué has few resources to police the 1,000,000 hectares for which he is responsible and he is not even sure he can trust some of his own staff. Recently his family was threatened with kidnapping if he didn't 'overlook' some illegal cutting going on in a remote area of his region. He is determined to do his job, but the temptation to 'turn a blind eye' is growing.

Tree-felling in progress

It is thought that about 6 million hectares of rainforest are logged annually in the tropics; that's 60,000 square kilometres – an area twice the size of Belgium. In 2006, the amount of logging in Southeast Asia and Central and South America was increasing, while in Africa it remained fairly constant.

In most cases, so-called 'clear-felling', in which all the trees are removed, does not take place, at least at first. Usually large, prime trees, such as mahogany and kapok, are selectively felled. Sometimes as few as two or three trees per hectare are cut. But there is always further damage as smaller trees are uprooted and crushed by the falling giant. Little is done to replace the trees or to allow natural regeneration. In Southeast Asia, much higher density removal takes place than in Central and South America or

'TURNING A BLIND EYE'

Even where governments attempt to regulate and control the logging companies, illegal logging still occurs without the knowledge of the governments concerned. Some governments even 'turn a blind eye' to these activities, either because officials are bribed by the logging companies not to report unlicensed logging, or because they lack the resources to police it effectively. It is estimated that illegal logging costs developing governments about US$10 billion annually in lost revenue, since the income goes to the illegal operators and not the country itself. The worst examples occur in the Amazon, Congo Basin and Indonesia.

Africa, and clear-felling often takes place. Poorly-designed logging roads damage watercourses (natural drainage) and cause soil erosion. Meanwhile, the intrusion of giant pieces of machinery results in changes in the forest ecosystem by frightening away birds and large mammals such as deer and jaguar.

Degradation to destruction

Although the logging itself may only damage, rather than destroy, the rainforest, this is only the beginning of the story. When the logging is finished, the farmers, agribusinesses, ranchers and fuelwood collectors move in to clear the land for other uses. The logging roads act as highways into the previously inaccessible forest, opening them up to further exploitation. In this way, the process of destruction is completed, and logging is the key to that destruction.

Making concessions

Logging itself can be a legitimate (and understandable) way for a country to obtain income from its natural resources. This is because governments often grant what are known as concessions (logging agreements) to logging companies. These are designed to regulate the amount of removal that takes place, but the concessions do not put a high enough value on the land. The areas of rainforest covered by the concessions are often in very remote regions and therefore difficult to police. The agreements usually apply for less than 10 years, which is far less time than it takes for the trees to be replaced. Without a long-term commitment, the company involved has no incentive to invest in proper forest management.

Only a few giant trees like this may be removed but many other smaller trees will be damaged as they fall. Cutting the creepers and lianas (climbing plants that often bind rainforest trees together) between the trees can prevent large specimens dragging others with them as they fall.

Planting trees - good idea, bad idea?

There are over 60 million hectares of tree plantations in developing countries. It seems to make sense to grow and farm trees like any other crop, but the reality is often rather different. In some areas, for example, parts of Brazil and Southeast Asia, large tracts of natural or primary forest have been cut down in order to plant faster-growing, more easily managed varieties, such as eucalyptus and acacia. Unlike natural forest, these 'single-species' plantations are more likely to be attacked by insect pests and cause depletion (impoverishment) of the soil.

Of course, it is not always the case that primary forest is removed. In Indonesia, for example, large areas of quick-growing forest have been planted in areas already cleared by logging

Controversial highways, such as this road through cleared palm plantation near Mirador, in Brazil, increases access to rainforests. By dividing the forests into smaller pieces their biodiversity is decreased, as animals are reluctant to cross the highways.

AREA OF TREE PLANTATION IN TROPICAL COUNTRIES		
Region	**Area of tree plantation (sq km)**	**% total forest cover**
Africa	80,000	4
Southeast Asia	1,160,000	62
Oceania	30,000	2
South America	100,000	6

Source: Forestry and Agriculture Organization (FAO/UN)

or lying fallow. Tree plantations provide a source of wood and fibre (for paper) that might otherwise come from natural forests. Rapidly growing forests are a good way of locking up CO_2 from the atmosphere, a process known as carbon sequestration. In this way, they can be an important way of combating global warming (see page 26). However, in the 'Top 10' deforesting countries (see table, page 11), plantation forests make up for less than 10 percent of the amount of natural forest lost.

Trouble down the mine

There are many other causes of rainforest destruction. Mining and exploring for oil cause deforestation locally. Large mines, like the Copperbelt mine in Zambia, once consumed large quantities of natural woodlands to supply fuel for smelting. Now, such mines are fed by plantation trees. Oil exploration using explosive devices, for example in Ecuador, not only destroys forests locally, but also opens them up to colonization by small or poor farmers. New roads, such as the Trans-Amazonian highway, also open up previously inaccessible forest to colonization and cattle ranchers. Main roads are soon followed by secondary roads, creating even better access. This adds 'value' to land, encouraging land buying and more deforestation.

DEBATE

You are in charge

You are speaking on behalf of an independent enquiry that was set up to decide whether countries with large areas of rainforest have the right to exploit this natural resource (or the resources it contains, such as minerals) without interference from the outside world. For which of these two courses of action do you argue in favour?

- We cannot control the actions of other states, even if we wanted to. They must be allowed to determine their own course of action.
- The issues are far too important to allow individual governments to decide; global action is needed, and needed quickly.

CHAPTER 4

A Valuable Resource

It is 2025 and in Congo, Central Africa, it has just been reported that the world's last remaining wild gorilla, outside zoos and conservation areas, has died. The final remaining population of lowland gorillas had been dwindling for years because habitat destruction, wars and illegal hunting for so-called 'bush meat' had all taken their toll. For many years the population had been too small to sustain itself and, despite reintroductions from captive gorillas, the decline continued. The few remaining gorillas spent their last years hounded by film crews and weakened by disease that had been brought about by contact with humans. Finally, only one remained, but he became ill and died on June 31, 2025.

Raiders of the lost ark

Gorillas still live in many parts of Central Africa, such as Congo and Equatorial Guinea, although they are under threat from all the pressures described above. Other 'great apes', like the orang-utan of Southeast Asia, are equally threatened. These animals are important because their survival depends on the survival of the rainforests, and the survival of the rainforests is crucial to the future of the Earth.

It is not hard to see why: 500 million people still live in and around rainforests, depending partly or entirely on them for food, fuelwood or other resources. Forest trees and plants are a global source of medicinal drugs, foods, building materials and many other products. They play a central role in regulating global weather patterns as well as influencing local climate, such as rainfall. Importantly, they prevent much of the Earth's soil from literally slipping into the sea. Rainforests also store vast quantities of carbon, which they have removed from the atmosphere as carbon dioxide, while producing a significant amount of the world's oxygen and rainfall. It may be that we are only just beginning to realize the vital role that rainforests can play in helping to combat global warming, so it is essential that we protect them.

BEATING DISEASE

In a Mexican rainforest, a species of wild maize (corn) has been found that is resistant to five of the world's seven most important corn viruses. It is now used to add resistance to corn crops worldwide. The rosy periwinkle plant from Madagascan forests provides a drug (vincristine) for treating leukaemia (a type of cancer), and the bark of a species of African cherry is now an important factor in the treatment of prostate cancer. Rainforest plants may also be a source of hope for future treatments of HIV/AIDS, Alzheimer's disease and malaria, all of which kill and disable millions of people each year. Rainforest animals are important here, too: vampire bats have a compound in their saliva that helps to prevent blood clots, and skin secretions from the poison arrow frog may be used as a painkiller.

Even in parks like this in Rwanda, gorillas, monkeys and other endangered species are constantly threatened by local wars and by gold and silver prospectors. Once mines are established, the mining crews are frequently fed 'bush meat' - local wild animals that are illegally hunted and killed wholesale in the mining areas.

Welcome to the gene pool

Most rainforests are very old. Some have hardly changed for tens of millions of years. The oldest rainforest in the world is Tama Negara, in Malaysia, estimated to be a staggering 130 million years old. That's 70 million years older than the last of the dinosaurs! They contain over 50 percent of all species of plants and animals on the planet, perhaps as much as 70 percent – which makes them the greatest living gene pool on Earth. It is this incredible variety or diversity of life – something we call biodiversity – that makes them so important.

Orang-utans live solitary lives in the forests of Indonesia and Malaysia: as well as destruction of their habitat, baby orang-utans are also taken from the wild to supply the trade in exotic pets; others are orphaned when their parents are killed for bush meat.

Going tropical

Tropical rainforests can be split into moist forests and equatorial forests. Moist forests are often in highlands, swathed in fog, mist and cloud. They are generally found further away from the Equator and receive about 130 centimetres of rainfall a year. They have a cooler, drier season, allowing sun to reach the forest floor as trees shed their leaves. This means they often have a well-developed 'understorey' (see page 22), not found in equatorial forest. Moist forests are found in parts of South America, North Australia, the Caribbean, West Africa and Southeast Asia – mainly Thailand, Burma, Vietnam and Sri Lanka.

Equatorial forests are found nearer the Equator. They receive more than 200 centimetres of rain, spread evenly throughout the year, and have the greatest biodiversity. Because of the lack of distinct seasons, the trees never lose all their leaves and little sunlight penetrates to the bare forest floor. These forests, found in the great Amazon Basin in South America, the Congo Basin in Central Africa, Indonesia, Malaysia and Papua New Guinea, make up about two-thirds of the world's tropical rainforests.

RAINFOREST BIODIVERSITY FACTFILE

- Rainforests cover less than 2 percent of the Earth's surface (including the oceans) but support more than 50 percent of all known life on the planet. They could contain up to 50 million species; many have yet to be named or even discovered.

- A tropical rainforest may have 500 different species of tree in a single hectare (100 metre x 100 metre square). A temperate forest in Europe or the USA will be dominated by only six or so species, and have 15 to 20 overall.

- Some trees can only be pollinated by a single type of insect, which is also dependent on the tree – if one dies, the other cannot survive.

- Where large-scale rainforest destruction is taking place, extinction rates in tropical rainforests are estimated to occur 100 times faster than natural rates.

All stop at the fifth floor

Rainforests can be thought of as multi-storey buildings, with different conditions and living opportunities (what are called 'niches') available to different plants and animals at every level. This is one of the reasons for their biodiversity. The main layer is the canopy, a dense 'ceiling' of leaves and branches that catches most of the sunlight and uses its energy to produce food (sugars) by photosynthesis. This layer therefore attracts the greatest number and variety of animals.

Above the canopy is the overstorey, the tops of taller (or emergent) trees that break through the canopy and may grow on a further 30 metres. Below the canopy is the understorey, which is a broken layer of smaller or juvenile trees and, below this, the shrub layer, which comprises shrubs and young trees that grow about 2–7 metres high. The lowest layer is the forest floor.

Down to the engine room

If the canopy is the powerhouse of the rainforest, the forest floor is the engine room. It is often surprisingly open, due to the lack of light penetrating the canopy and lower layers. In fact, something like 70–90 percent of life in the rainforest is found in the trees, but this does not mean that nothing is growing on the floor – there is a complex community of insects, fungi and bacteria, which ensure that the nutrient cycle is continued. The hot,

In this primary forest, the canopy is so dense that little or no light penetrates through to the forest floor. Consequently, very little grows there and most of the life of the forest is concentrated in the upper reaches of the trees.

humid conditions mean that fallen leaves and other dead material are completely decomposed (broken down) and recycled back into plant material in a matter of days. Whole trees may disappear in weeks in this way.

The combination of strong sunlight, high rainfall and rapid decomposition means that rainforests are highly productive places. When a forest tree falls, seedlings on the forest floor compete to fill the available space, growing at rates of 5–10 centimetres a day, to out-compete each other. Perhaps surprisingly, however, nutrients are recycled so rapidly in rainforests that the soil itself is often quite thin and nutrient-poor, which is one of the factors that makes them vulnerable to destruction.

Past, present and future

Although we cannot stop the use of rainforests completely, as so many people rely on it for their livelihoods, we can improve the way they are used, and try to lessen the more damaging effects. In doing this, we must think long term and try to make our use of rainforests sustainable – this means that we have to use their abundant resources in a way that does not damage them now, or in the future.

DEBATE

You are in charge
You are responsible for setting up a conservation programme in a protected area of rainforest in Central Africa. You have to convince your donors that your ideas will safeguard wildlife *without* damaging local communities. Which argument do you support?

- It is important to concentrate on protecting key species, like gorillas, since they indicate the overall health of an ecosystem as well as generating sympathy and support from the public.
- You have to understand and manage the ecosystem as a whole, including the people who live there; this may mean that key species are still killed for food, even though this may be unpopular with supporters of the project.

CHAPTER 5

The Climate Shifts

It is 2020 and this is an extract from an article written by the environment correspondent of the new international paper *Global News*. "I am standing in the middle of what was once a rainforest in the Malaysian peninsula. What strikes you most is not the heat (which is intense), but the fact that most of the trees are dead or dying, not this time because of chainsaws, but because it is simply too hot for them to survive. What scientists have been predicting for the past 20 years is now a reality. We have not heeded the warnings to cut down on our use of fossil fuels like oil and gas. Carbon dioxide emissions have hardly altered, despite agreements made back in the 1990s to make significant reductions. Now we can see one of the results – thousands of trees dying of heat stress."

The effects of such changes are not just higher temperatures, but also change in climate patterns across the world. Forests are especially sensitive to climate change, so by 2020 one-third of all remaining rainforests really will be under threat from higher temperatures. It is likely that large areas of 'die-off' will have been spotted by satellite images across most of the tropics. Southeast Asia in particular may be prone to widespread forest fires, partly resulting from the rapidly drying conditions.

The weather makers

Rainforests make weather, because the canopy of each tree recycles over 700 litres of water back into the atmosphere every day – that's nearly 200,000 litres for every hectare of forest. Large rainforests contribute to the formation of rain clouds, and can generate as much as 75 percent of their own rain. Forests also contribute to something called 'surface albedo'. This means that they absorb more heat than bare soil. Removing rainforests increases the amount that the Earth's surface reflects the Sun's heat, causing a warming effect. This in turn affects global weather by altering wind and ocean currents. Global

This rainforest fire in Mexico may have been caused by the forest's reduction in size, which significantly decreased its local rainfall. Rainforests create their own weather, accounting for as much as three-quarters of their rainfall, so less forest means less rain – and more fires.

weather patterns may become more unstable and extreme as a direct result of rainforest destruction.

Warning signs

Since the mid-1990s, rainforests worldwide have experienced periods of severe drought. In 1997, forests in South Asia burned for weeks as the drought struck. The drought occurred again in 2005, this time also being repeated in the Amazon. Forest fires themselves further decrease rainfall as the smoke particles interfere with droplet formation. The causes of droughts are still a matter of fierce debate. Many people believe, however, that they are the signs of global climate change and particularly the trend known as global warming.

AMPHIBIANS FEEL THE STRAIN

Amphibians, such as frogs, toads and newts, are especially sensitive to temperature changes in the water. Their ponds may be drying out as a result of climate change. Amphibian populations are generally declining throughout the world. During the last 20 years in the Australian rainforest, for example, at least 14 species of stream-dwelling frog have disappeared or declined by more than 90 percent. In Costa Rica, the brightly coloured Monteverde golden toad has not been seen since 1989, following two years of unusually low rainfall.

The carbon trap

Rainforests play an important role in sequestering (locking up) carbon dioxide (CO_2) in their vegetation, during photosynthesis. They may, therefore, be important in regulating the amount of CO_2 in the atmosphere. Of course, they also produce CO_2 as they respire, in exactly the same way that animals do, but the balance between respiration and photosynthesis depends on many factors. In general, however, newly growing or expanding forests act as carbon 'sinks', trapping large amounts of CO_2 for the lifetime of the tree, until it decays. It is calculated that reforesting 1 million square kilometres of land would sequester more than 10 billion tonnes of CO_2 by 2050; this is a year's total human production of carbon dioxide. At any one time, forests contain nearly as much carbon (in the form of wood and vegetation) as is present in the entire atmosphere. They are second in importance only to the oceans in storing and recycling CO_2.

Burning issues

What is certain is that when forests are burned, degraded or cleared, sequestration is reversed, as large amounts of CO_2 are released into the atmosphere – along with other 'greenhouse' gases, such as methane. The burning of forests liberates about 2 billion tonnes of CO_2 into the atmosphere each year; that's over 20 percent of all synthetic emissions. Clearing and burning forests therefore directly contributes to global warming and climate change.

The way of life of the people living in the Central African Republic rainforest has hardly changed in thousands of years. They carry a deep knowledge and understanding of the rainforest itself, which has been passed on through many generations.

Cause and effect

Scientists cannot agree on what the future levels of CO_2 in the atmosphere might be. Most think that the increase in CO_2 will lead to a rise in temperature of several degrees across the world, by 2020. This in turn will lead to changes in global weather patterns, such as increases in droughts, hurricanes and changes in rainfall in many parts of the world. Sea levels are also likely to rise, increasing the risk of flooding to low-lying areas, such as the Maldives. The effect of such changes on rainforests is hard to predict. In the Amazon, temperatures are likely to rise, resulting in drier forests and a shift of savannah vegetation nearer the Equator. Drier soils will mean changes in the composition of the canopy, in turn affecting the species that live there, for example, trees may simply die of heat stress. In Africa, regular seasonal rain patterns may be disrupted, again reducing overall rainfall in equatorial areas. If rain stops falling, large areas of forest will become arid scrubland. Low levels of rainfall in the centre of West African countries are already being blamed on excessive clearing of coastal rainforests. Deforestation leads to declining rainfall; declining rainfall leads to deforestation. Global warming could lead to both.

DEBATE

You are a climate change scientist making a presentation to world leaders at a meeting arranged by the United Nations. The previous speaker, a popular biologist, has argued that the threats to rainforests of global warming are exaggerated, and that plants and animals will adapt to the changing conditions.

Courses of action:
- You agree that climate change is a cause for concern, but argue that there are many more urgent threats to rainforests, such as land clearance and logging, that need to be dealt with first.
- You argue that rainforest destruction and climate change are closely linked and that the two issues must be addressed together as a matter of priority.

CHAPTER 6

A Dwindling Race?

It is 2020. The following is an extract taken from an audio-recording of Katunga, an elder of the Yekuana tribe in southern Venezuela, shortly before the tribe was attacked by gold miners. During the attack several members of the tribe, including Katunga, were killed. "There are few of us left now and most of us are old. The young no longer want a life working in our forest gardens and hunting for bush meat. They think they can make a better life for themselves in the big city and don't want to listen to their elders. When we die, who will carry on our traditions and look after the forest? Even now, our land is attacked on all sides from those who would take its riches but not care for its future. We hear our brothers, the Kayapo and the Iban, have gone. Only two nights ago the gold hunters came while we were eating in the *maloca* (communal dwelling) and threatened us with guns and clubs. We are afraid they will return and, with our young men gone, who will protect us?"

A way of life

It is estimated that 500 million people live in or at the edge of the world's tropical rainforests. They depend on the forests for many commodities such as food, firewood and water. Of these forest-dependent people, about 50 million are native or indigenous peoples who rely entirely on the forests for their way of life. They know the ways of the forest and do not over-exploit it, gathering food from small garden plots, which are shifted every few years, or hunting and fishing in ways that do not threaten the resource itself. The forest not only meets their immediate needs of food and shelter – it also forms part of their culture and tradition. You might say they live in the forest – but the forest also lives in them.

Now that way of life is changing, because, as forests fall, indigenous people lose not just their homes but also their culture, their rituals, even their history. With this goes a vast store of knowledge about how rainforests work – the healing properties of its plants, forest cultivation methods, even the understanding of its ecology.

ESTIMATED INDIGENOUS POPULATION IN SOUTH AMERICAN COUNTRIES

Country	Number of different groups (tribes or ethnic groups)	Estimated population (2005)
Bolivia	31	171,000
Brazil	200	213,000
Colombia	52	70,000
Ecuador	6	95,000
Guyana	9	40,000
Peru	60	300,000
Suriname	5	7,500
Venezuela	16	387,000

Source: Rhett Butler 2005 (rainforests.mongabay.com)

A tribesperson plays a traditional instrument (a *sape*) at a world music festival in Borneo. Cultures like these may be lost if rainforest destruction continues at the present rate.

Attack from all sides

The decline of rainforest tribes is not just a matter of removal of the forests – it is more complex than that. As rainforests have been opened up by loggers, gold prospectors, farmers and other settlers, the way of life of many of the indigenous people has been changed forever, even where they remain in their traditional areas. Many have fallen victim to new diseases such as pneumonia and TB, against which they had no protection. Others have been harassed or even

Images like this, of a rainforest Amerindian making the most of new business opportunities, show how rainforest people can adapt to a changing world. If this change is to be successful, it is important that traditional rainforest cultures and values are preserved within a more modern setting.

killed by ranchers who wanted their land. Some have drifted from the forests to find work in cities or on government-backed agricultural schemes, but their different background and culture has made it hard for them to integrate into these new societies. Often they have been shunned and seen as outcasts. The result has often been alcoholism or other social problems, such as addiction to gambling. Many have tried to return to life in the forest, but their lives have changed so much they are now caught between two cultures. Also, it is often the case that the forest they once lived in no longer exists.

A TRAGIC END BUT A NEW BEGINNING?

In 2005, the tragic murder of an American nun, Dorothy Stang, highlighted many of the issues that confront indigenous people. The elderly nun worked to protect the rights and interests of small farmers and indigenous people in the Brazilian state of Pará. She was killed by two men, allegedly working for a local cattle rancher who resented her support for local farmers. Her assassination led the Brazilian President, Luiz da Silva, to send 2,000 troops to the area to safeguard local forests and their people.

A changing culture

Just as damaging, in some ways, is the fact that their culture itself has been changed by these outside influences. Indeed, many are happy to take on the trappings of the outside society. For example, modern dress such as T-shirts and sunglasses are now commonplace among rainforest people, particularly in the Amazon Basin. Modern metal cooking utensils are often preferred over traditional earthenware. Many now have outboard motors to power their canoes and dugouts.

In many ways, this is to be expected, even welcomed. The forest way of life is tough and sometimes brutal. It is easy to glamorize a forest existence, when the reality is often very different. For example, local wars may break out between neighbouring tribes and life expectancy is often short.

A clash of ideas

Recently, many tribes have entered into deals with big companies who are keen to exploit their land for logging or mineral extraction. Sometimes both can benefit, but more often the indigenous people lose out. For example, in Papua New Guinea, Bahineimo tribesmen sold off their land to a logging company, but it later emerged that many of the signatures on the agreement had been forged. Sometimes high-ranking tribal members, or elders, are influenced or even tricked into persuading their people to part with land. Occasionally there is a clash between the older members of a tribe, who want to keep things as they are, and the younger members, who want to see the development of their land for logging or plantations. Some governments encourage these developments, since they see this as economically good for the country; a few still refuse to even recognize the land rights (ownership) of their indigenous people.

A new way forward?

The picture is not totally bleak, however. Partly through international pressure, many countries with indigenous people are beginning to recognize their rights. Instead of being encouraged to

DEBATE

You are an adviser to the Brazilian government during its efforts to preserve its indigenous people, while still allowing exploitation of its rainforests. Here are two possible courses of action:

■ The government acknowledges the importance and value of preserving rainforest people's traditional way of life, and recognizes that the only way of doing so is to create more reserves and protected areas, using force, if necessary, to protect them.

■ The government accepts that it is unrealistic for rainforest tribes to go on living in traditional ways; it must invest in their integration into modern society through education and much greater financial help, in such a way that their essential culture and character is not lost.

A coffee farmer in Nicaragua checks the quality of his coffee cherries (the berry surrounding the bean). Rainforests can be a continued source of income for local people by creating business opportunities based on natural forest resources, such as coffee trees.

migrate to the cities or onto agricultural land, some rainforest people are being helped to continue living in a traditional way, while also earning an income through work. This can be achieved by creating reserves on their original land, allowing small businesses and enterprises to run alongside a more traditional way of life. Not all indigenous people want this kind of existence, however.

In Brazil indigenous peoples have been recognized as having permanent legal title (rights) to 11 percent of the land. Even so, while some better-known tribes, such as the Yanomami in northern Brazil and southern Venezuela, have absolute rights over 83,000 square kilometres of protected reserve, few others have such full recognition. There are about 1,000 rainforest tribes, worldwide. We do not yet know if most, perhaps all, of these will gradually die out or be slowly absorbed into the outside world.

CHAPTER 7

Turning the Tide

It is 2045. Extract from an article written by the editor of the international newspaper *Global News*: "Twenty-five years ago, as a young reporter, I visited this rainforest in Malaysia and reported that it was dying. Today it is a different story, not only here, but worldwide. Despite continued losses of rainforest in the 2020s and early 2030s, the tide seems to have turned. Some countries have seen increases in forested areas, although it will take many more years for the trees to become fully mature. Many species that were once close to extinction in the wild have been saved, including the lowland gorilla, which is now thriving in many central African countries, like Chad. Many tropical countries like this one, through a combination of international aid and their own efforts, have healthy and expanding forests. These countries are providing resources for themselves, while generating income from tourism and the export of forest products. The local forest tribes here are combining many of their traditional ways of hunting and growing food with successful small enterprises, such as the branding and marketing of forest-based cosmetics and pharmaceuticals. Although it may still be too early to be sure, the world may have woken up just in time to save its most precious resource."

Statistics, statistics...

One problem with monitoring rainforest destruction is the reliance on statistics supplied by government, institutes and other authorities. There can be discrepancies, for example, in 2002, the Brazilian government announced that the rate of rainforest destruction in the Amazon had fallen by 13 percent – an area of 15,787 square kilometres had been destroyed by logging and forest fires, compared to 18,226 square kilometres the previous year. The government claimed that this was due to increased monitoring of illegal activities, and better land use. However, satellite images produced in 2003 by Brazil's National Institute of Space Research suggested that almost

25,000 square kilometres had been cleared. In both the following years it was about the same. It is hard to say which figures are more accurate; they may both be true since data like these often depend on exact definitions and meanings of rainforest and of its destruction. The FAO (Food and Agriculture Organization), part of the United Nations, believes that destruction overall decreased slightly in the period 2000–2005 compared with the previous five years. Others, however, disagree.

Small steps

There is some good news, however. Thailand has banned logging in its country since 1988. Costa Rica has now protected 26 percent of its country in national parks and reserves. In 2005 the Brazilian federal parliament passed a law on the management of public (government-owned) forests, setting out how forests are to be allocated for sustainable use, involving both private companies and local communities. Perhaps these are small signs that attitudes towards protecting the world's rainforests are beginning to change, and the issue is being taken more seriously.

A hiker crosses the Arenal Hanging Bridges in the rainforest near the Arenal Volcano in Costa Rica. Rainforests enrich all our lives, so we all have a responsibility to ensure that they continue to flourish.

TAKING ACTION

We cannot just close rainforests off and put a giant 'keep out' sign on the fence. Rainforests are a resource and they can bring benefit to millions of people worldwide. There are five main ways in which we can do something:

- establish more parks and reserves to protect the really important bits of rainforests and the wildlife they can contain.
- restore damaged and cleared forests, and plant trees so that new forests do not have to be cut down.
- help people to live in ways that are less damaging to the environment - in particular this means tackling poverty.
- encourage (and support) big business, such as the timber industry, to operate in ways that greatly reduce damage to the forests - this means that both governments and the industries themselves have to monitor and change forest practices so that they are more sustainable.
- be involved personally, and encourage others to be.

A walk in the park

Creating more parks and reserves, especially in areas with a very high diversity or rarity of species, is necessary. Already many exist, ranging from completely protected areas, where damaging operations such as logging and other activities are prohibited, to areas in which people both live and work. Success is more likely if the rainforest generates income for local communities, for example, by employing locals as guides or making handicrafts. Where this is not possible, the benefits must still be apparent, for example, by allowing (and encouraging) the sustainable use of forest products. In this way, local people are more likely to be involved in protecting these areas, by looking out for poachers or illegal logging. Currently, about 8 percent of rainforests are protected to some extent, but many experts now believe this needs to be increased to at least 20 percent.

A SUCCESS STORY

Xingu Park was formed in 1991 as a means of safeguarding the Menkragnoti Kayapo people's land and culture. With help from international and other groups, an area the size of Belgium (about 30,000 square kilometres) was established in the Amazon Basin to allow them to continue and develop their way of life. Crucial to its success was a long-term plan to manage its borders effectively against logging companies, miners, cattle ranchers and commercial fishermen. Now the community provides bilingual education and opportunities to develop income for its members. A satellite map of the area shows widespread deforestation around its borders, but almost none within. However, conservation must ensure that continuous stretches of rainforest – not just isolated islands – are protected, otherwise they can degrade very quickly.

People of the Kayapo tribe at Xingu Park take part in a tribal dance in a protected area of their traditional lands. Generally it is better to allow local people to continue to live and work in these areas. In this way, they are more likely to protect the areas themselves.

This fruit bat, and birds like parrots, are important in spreading rainforest seeds and may therefore help to speed up the restoration of the cleared land.

LEAVING IT TO THE BIRDS AND THE BATS

Planting fast-growing fruit trees, like figs, may attract birds, such as parrots and macaws, and fruit bats back into deforested areas. It is hoped that the seeds (from nearby forested areas) in the animals' droppings will allow the gradual reintroduction of native species, such as figs, bananas, avocado and mango. Even trees with larger seeds, like mahogany, can be spread by some pigeon-like birds. Both birds and bats are important pollinators - this may eventually help to restore the area's biodiversity.

Restoring land and planting trees

It takes hundreds, perhaps thousands, of years for a rainforest to become established. We can't just bring them back, but we can make the best possible use of the areas already cleared or damaged. To do this we must increase the productivity of farms, cattle pasture and plantations that exist on land that was once rainforest. For example, it is possible to grow higher-yielding crops or grasses that will grow well on degraded forest soils. What has become scrubland (land now covered in small trees and bushes) can be restored by tree planting and better management. Crucially, this will reduce the need to clear more forest.

Restoring ecosystems is most likely to succeed in regions where parts of the original forest still remain. Small clearings recover quickly by themselves, while larger areas need more careful reforestation (replanting). Secondary forests are much lower in biodiversity than natural or primary forest, but will still encourage the return of some species of wildlife. Just as importantly, the newly forested areas can be used for the sustainable harvest of forest products, such as fruits and nuts, as well as timber. It is estimated that tree plantations of fast-growing species could meet the entire world's demand for pulpwood (for paper) on 3 percent of the world's already cleared forests. Meanwhile, planting slower-growing, indigenous (native) shrub and tree species in other areas will help to restore biodiversity over longer periods of time.

Cutting carbon

Replanted forest will also absorb large amounts of CO_2 and sequester the carbon for the lifetime of the tree, or longer (see Chapter 5). Doubling the rate of forest planting over the next 30 years would provide a 'carbon sink' big enough to absorb one-eighth of current world CO_2 emissions, instead of releasing it into the Earth's atmosphere. In Malaysia, there is a project to restore 25,000 hectares of logged rainforest with tree species that are suited to grow on degraded land, together with species that will yield marketable forest fruits. Similar projects are taking place in Uganda and Ecuador.

DEBATE

You are taking over the management of a rainforest reserve on the Indonesian island of Borneo. The previous manager adopted a 'keep people out' approach, banning any form of exploitation of the reserve. This was unpopular with local people and expensive to police, but the forest remained largely unharmed. You favour a more inclusive approach in which people can benefit too, but you are concerned that it will be difficult to control.

Courses of action:
- You decide that the risks of allowing greater access to the reserve are too great and continue the present policy of exclusion – after all, you can always change things later!
- You decide to allow people to return slowly after talking to local leaders, even though there are risks, and some initial damage to the forest is inevitable.

CHAPTER 8

Value-added Rainforests

It is 2020: at a rock concert to save the rainforests being staged in the new Olympic Stadium in Rio de Janeiro. The line-up has been spectacular and there have been many messages of support from bands and politicians alike. Suddenly, a small, elderly figure appears on the stage. He is the chief of the local Kayapo tribe. This is part of what he says to a silent crowd. "My friends, you may wonder what I have to say to you that has not already been said. In truth, I find it hard to know myself. I only know what my heart tells me. The forest is part of the Earth. When we destroy it, part of the Earth dies too. When we protect it, the Earth breathes more easily. How can this happen? Only when we value it for itself and not simply as land for our crops, or cattle, or timber, or gold. All these things it can give us, but only if we let it live, let it grow, let it prosper. This is what I ask – not only for my people, but for the people of the world. The rainforest can be our future. This is my message to you all. Thank you."

Helping people to help themselves

Many of the people in rural areas live off the land, making use of whatever is available, whatever the cost – including the destruction of forests. Governments often find it difficult to balance their people's – and their country's – immediate needs against the longer-term need to conserve their rainforests. One approach is to help the rural poor help themselves by improving and 'intensifying' current ways of farming – a system known as agroforestry. This includes growing a greater range of crops, allowing access to new markets, while also improving the soil. This type of farming can exist alongside, or even within, natural forest, allowing trees and other woodland products to be harvested as well as crops and even livestock.

Without ownership of or 'title' to a piece of land, there is little encouragement for poor farmers to maintain or improve the land on

This Madagascan rainforest is part of a national forest programme (NFP). Such programmes bring together different interest groups and international agencies, achieving a more sustainable approach to rainforests.

which they work – it is easier to move on and clear more forested land. But ownership is difficult to achieve for people with little or no money – this is why local (or micro) credit facilities may be a good idea. These kinds of facilities allow farmers to borrow, and later, save, in order to acquire land. They also encourage a sense of business or entrepreneurship, and they can also give people a greater sense of identity and dignity.

Tackling big business

Unlike local agriculture, such as growing indigenous fruits and vegetables, like squash, cassava and yams, large-scale farming is difficult to manage within natural forest environments. This is because large-scale farming is run by big businesses and corporations that exploit the forests. However, by reducing or stopping the use of chemical pesticides and fertilizers, the pollution of land and watercourses could be reduced, and the health of the labourers improved. Alternative natural methods of pest control could be used instead. Strips of forest between plantations can act as 'corridors' that connect sections of forest and reduce the loss of biodiversity. These corridors also act as natural protection for the plantations, reducing wind and storm damage, soil loss, and the spread of disease.

A STEP IN THE RIGHT DIRECTION

Many rainforest countries are now adopting environmental plans to combat the harmful effects of deforestation in their own land. In 1996, Mexico announced its first national programme to save the last remaining 10 percent of its forests. In 2006, Madagascar introduced a new scheme to create protected areas that allow some resource use, such as limited removal of trees for timber to help reduce poverty. Small steps, such as removing the secrecy around bids for logging contracts, and simplifying land ownership, may also go a long way to helping rainforest countries produce more successful plans.

Sustainable logging - the impossible dream?

Can logging itself be sustainable? The idea is still a controversial one. Many ecologists believe it is impossible to take large trees from rainforests in a sustainable way because a mature tree can take up to 100 years to grow. Few companies are prepared to wait that long for their next crop and, even if they were, the area of forest needed to support this kind of regeneration time would just be unrealistic. To make tropical timber production sustainable, however, we may

Much of the damage caused by logging is to other trees, as prize specimens are removed. This innovative use of helicopters to remove felled trees reduces both the direct damage and the need for large access roads.

have to invest in the greater development of fast-growing, high-yielding timber plantations on land that has already been cleared of natural forest.

Where logging of natural forest does take place, companies need to ensure that removal of trees is carried out with minimum damage to the environment, such as airlifting trees. Ideally, trees should be replaced or allowed to regenerate naturally, which could be enforced through international and local laws. Tougher measures against corruption of officials and the forgery of documents claiming that timber has been produced sustainably could be put in place. Financial and other incentives (rewards) could be made available to countries that make sure this happens.

Everybody counts

Most people are aware of rainforest destruction but feel there is little they can do, which is untrue. We can all do things – both individually and as part of groups – no matter how small they may seem. These include supporting organizations that campaign for rainforests, but also influencing those around us – our families for instance – in what we do and buy. For example, there are now many food and cosmetic products that are developed from rainforest sources. These ensure that local farmers or indigenous people receive a guaranteed proportion of profits directly, rather than the tiny amounts allowed them by big companies who buy their products at low prices and then make large profits themselves. These products are often distinctively labelled or can be sourced through the Internet. When buying tropical wood products, it is essential to make sure the wood has come from a non-damaging supplier and you can do this by looking for recognized, international labelling systems, such as the FSC (Forest Stewardship Council) scheme, which means that the wood you buy has come from properly managed forests.

A BETTER WAY OF DOING THINGS

Logging provides work for 100,000 people in Sarawak (part of Malaysia) and generates US$1.5 billion annually in exports. Currently, only 1 percent of the area used for logging worldwide is managed and only 0.1 percent is managed sustainably. In the meantime, many developing countries are already getting much greater value from their timber by 'processing' it before export – this means making it into much more valuable sawn wood, such as planks, panels, and other wood products. According to the International Tropical Timber Organization (ITTO), Africa now processes 80 percent of its logs itself, Asia 92 percent, and South America, nearly 100 percent. Higher value can relieve the pressure on rainforests by making those areas that are harvested even more profitable.

A new value?

The most important of the underlying factors that lead to rainforest destruction (see Chapter 2) are poverty and debt in the countries involved. Therefore, we need to find a way of increasing the value of rainforests standing, and reducing the value of a rainforest that is cut to the ground. In order to be effective, these measures would need to benefit the economy and welfare of the particular country.

At present governments often offer incentives (such as 'tax breaks') that encourage the conversion of rainforest, say, for logging or agriculture. This gives them income over the short term. It also means they can claim they are 'developing' their country's resources. Removing these incentives and changing development policies to ones that recognize the true, long-term value of rainforests would make destructive practices less attractive. This value would take into account, for example, the huge capacity of rainforests to prevent soil erosion or regulate water supply. One possibility is for rich countries to pay rainforest countries 'carbon credits' that recognize the value of forests in combating global warming.

A raft of measures

The rate of destruction might be slowed if the (shifting cultivator) poor or small farmers (as a collective) are allowed space and protection from new settlers, in order to continue their way of life. Loans and better training might also help. More efficient use of already cleared or damaged land could do the same. So too, would

Eco-tourism is one way of ensuring that rainforests are more valuable to a country when standing. But it is important that such activity does not damage the environment and that local people benefit. Sensitive development and involvement of the local community can help to achieve this.

better marketing of 'non-wood' forest products such as nuts, fruits and especially pharmaceuticals – a practice sometimes called bio-prospecting. In Costa Rica, an agreement with an American pharmaceutical company means that a percentage of profits from successful rainforest compounds goes to the conservation of forests. Increased eco-tourism that does not damage the environment is another way of adding value to a standing – rather than a cleared – rainforest.

Facing up to responsibilities

At the same time, the rich countries have to recognize that they have already benefited from almost unlimited access to the rainforest resources of poorer countries – and now it is time to pay. A way of doing so may be to cancel much of the debt owed by poor countries to the rich nations and international banks.

None of these changes will occur easily or overnight – they will require co-operation between international and national agencies and governments, and, most importantly, between governments and local communities. Only two things are certain, however: we are all involved, and none of us can afford to do nothing.

DEBATE

You are a young person looking forward to a long and happy life. You are naturally concerned about issues like rainforests, since you understand that they affect your future. But there are many other important things in your life and it's hard to see what you alone can do about rainforest destruction.

Courses of action:
- Leave it to others; there are people with much more power and influence than you who can change things.
- Understand that you have power and influence too; what you say, what you do, who you vote for in future, all have an effect – even on issues that seem as big and difficult to resolve as rainforest destruction.

Glossary

billion Generally accepted to be one thousand million

biodiversity The diversity or variety of plants and animals found in a particular habitat or area. A high biodiversity is often seen as a sign of a healthy ecosystem since it contains plenty of genetic variation.

biomass The total amount (mass) of plant and animal material found in a particular area.

carbon sequestration The trapping of the carbon in carbon dioxide in plant material (leaves, stems, trunks, etc.) as a way of removing it from the atmosphere.

concessions Permits granted by governments, normally to big companies, to exploit forests and other natural resources. The government concerned gets useful income, but often exerts too little control over the use or management of the resource.

conservation The management of habitats or species to ensure their survival. Conservation may therefore involve using or exploiting a resource (such as rainforest) in order to protect it.

decomposition The breakdown of animal and plant remains by the action of small invertebrates, fungi and bacteria.

deforestation Removal of forest, usually through human activity. This may be because of logging, clearing for agriculture, fire or other reasons.

degradation Damage caused to forests, for example, by removing some, but not all, trees; often followed by more complete destruction as other users take over.

developing countries Countries that are relatively poor and which rely mainly on agriculture and the exploitation of primary resources (timber, minerals, etc.) for their economy.

development How a country or region develops, particularly economically, for example, through increasing industry. Development can sometimes harm the environment, but does not always need to do so (see sustainable development).

ecosystem All the interdependent factors, such as water, nutrients, vegetation, wildlife and so on, that make up a viable (working) habitat such as rainforest.

eco-tourism Tourism specifically aimed at allowing visitors to experience wildlife and natural habitats. This can be a very valuable source of income and jobs for local people, but may damage the habitats themselves in the process.

environmental impact The effect of a development project on the surrounding area or environment. For example, dam building frequently results in the flooding of large areas of forest, and the eviction of indigenous people.

fallow (period) Time when cleared or farmed land is left uncultivated to allow nutrients to return naturally or by growing certain plants (e.g, plants of the pea family) that add nutrients through their roots.

foreign debt Money owed by poorer countries to rich countries or banks. The reason for these loans may be to help their development, but may also be to pay for arms. Just paying back the interest on these loans can take up a large part of a poor country's annual earnings.

hectare An area equivalent to a square 100 metres by 100 metres. There are 100 hectares in a square kilometre.

indigenous Refers to any people (or plants and animals) that are the original (or native) inhabitants of an area. Where it refers to people, the term is usually associated with well-established traditions and ways of life (cultures).

niche A particular part of an ecosystem, such as the rainforest canopy, offering particular opportunities (for example, food or shelter) to certain kinds of animals or plants.

nutrients Simple substances, such as nitrates and phosphates, made available to plants by the process of decomposition.

primary forest Original or native forest, largely free from human activity and usually very diverse.

regeneration The process of regrowth of an area's vegetation; may occur naturally or be speeded up by planting of trees.

savannah Mixed grassland and trees found north and south of rainforest areas and generally drier in climate; like rainforests, however, often a target for ranching and grazing.

secondary forest Planted or naturally regenerated forest growing on cleared primary forest. Secondary forest usually has a much lower biodiversity than primary forest, but can still be important both economically and ecologically.

shifting cultivation A traditional form of agriculture in which land is cleared and farmed for a time, before the farmers move on. The soil is allowed to recover naturally so that it can be farmed again (known as lying fallow).

subsidy Payment to companies or businesses, usually by governments, which encourages a particular development, such as logging or agriculture. Subsidies therefore mask the true cost of the development.

surface albedo The degree to which the Earth's surface reflects or absorbs the Sun's energy. Cutting down rainforests increases surface albedo, which means that more of the Sun's energy is reflected, altering weather patterns and ocean currents.

sustainable development Development of a country or region that brings economic and social benefits, but does not damage the environment or its ability to sustain people now and in the future.

tax breaks Reductions in tax; usually awarded to businesses, to encourage them to invest in development such as logging or agriculture.

World Bank International institution that lends money to countries to enable them to develop their resources, such as minerals, water and forests. Often criticized for not insisting that proper analysis of the environmental impact of these projects is carried out.

Further Information

Books

Deep Jungle by by Fred Pearce (Eden Books, Transworld, 2005)

Go M.A.D! – Go Make A Difference: over 500 Daily Ways to Save the Planet by Jo Bourne (Think Publishing Ltd, 2003)

Rainforest People by Edward Parker (Hodder Wayland, 2002)

The Vanishing Rainforest by Richard Platt (Frances Lincoln Publishers, 2003)

Websites

www.focusonrainforests.co.uk
Gives information and activities on rainforests for 11–14 year olds.

www.forests.org
Website of the Rainforest Information Centre; acts as a portal to other rainforest sites.

www.mongabay.com
Gives up-to-date information and statistics on all aspects of rainforests, much of it based on United Nations (FAO) figures.

www.rainforestconcern.org
Gives information about, and campaigns for, the saving of rainforests, particularly in Ecuador.

www.rainforestfoundationuk.org
Website of Rainforest Foundation UK, which supports indigenous people and others who live in rainforests.

www.ran.org
Website of the Rainforest Action Network, a US-based organization that campaigns for the sustainable use of rainforests worldwide.

www.survival-international.org
Provides information and campaigns for the survival of rainforest and other indigenous people.

www.wwf.org.uk
Website of the World Wide Fund for Nature: produces information and educational material on rainforests and other habitats.

Debate Panel answers

Page 7:
It is certainly true that this is a matter that affects your future. But this is not always the best way to get your point across. Arguing that this is a real-life issue that is highly relevant to your education (in all kinds of ways) may therefore be the best approach.

Page 13:
It may be tempting to try to maximize your income from the company by simply charging them more. But this will not address the real problem of deforestation. You might insist that the company invests in rainforest conservation, while still allowing them access to other land. You should be prepared to drive a much harder bargain that will ultimately benefit your people – and the rainforest – more.

Page 17:
It is true we cannot, or should not, control the actions of other states. However, richer countries are in a strong position to help and encourage rainforest nations to save their forests in many ways. Examples of this include cancelling debt, beneficial trade agreements and investing heavily in rainforest conservation programmes.

Page 23:
There is no easy answer to this question. It is true that a healthy gorilla population probably also indicates a healthy ecosystem. But the best way to ensure this happens might not be simply to protect gorillas! It may be better to concentrate on managing the area as a whole, while ensuring the gorilla population overall is not endangered. This may not go down well with your supporters and you will have to be prepared to explain the reasoning behind your approach. But you didn't take on the job to be popular!

Page 27:
It is unlikely that most species will be able to adapt quickly enough to avoid the effects of global warming. On the other hand, there are possibly more immediate threats to rainforests (and therefore species), particularly land clearance. Ultimately, however, global warming may pose the greatest threat; and it will also take the longest time to reverse. We should therefore address both issues now as a matter of great urgency.

Page 32:
Both approaches may be appropriate, depending on the particular area and tribes involved. In the end, however, change is inevitable, and is often lead by tribal people themselves. You will have seen examples in this book where tribal lands have been recognized at the same time as encouraging certain kinds of development, such as setting up small businesses, better health care and education.

Page 39:
You will have to make your own decision, based on local circumstances. Whatever you decide, you will need to talk to local leaders and others before making a decision. What is certain is that you will need their co-operation regardless of which plan of action you put into effect.

Page 45:
This one really is your decision! No one can force you to do anything. There are many calls on your time and energy, and rainforests may not be top of your list. It is worth remembering, however, you do have power – as a 'consumer', as a member of different groups (your school, clubs, etc.) and, quite soon, as a voter. How you use this influence is up to you – but many would argue, it should be used!

Index

Page numbers in **bold** refer to illustrations.